Discordant

by Richard Hamilton

AUTUMN
HOUSE PRESS
Pittsburgh, PA

Autumn House Press is a nonprofit corporation
whose mission is the publication and promotion
of poetry and other fine literature. The press
gratefully acknowledges support from individ-
ual donors, public and private foundations, and
government agencies. This book was supported,
in part, by the Greater Pittsburgh Arts Council
through its Allegheny Arts Revival Grant and the
Pennsylvania Council on the Arts, a state agency funded by the Commonwealth
of Pennsylvania, and the National Endowment for the Arts. To find out more
about how National Endowment for the Arts grants impact individuals and com-
munities, visit www.arts.gov.

Library of Congress Cataloging-in-Publication Data

Names: Hamilton, Richard, 1975- author
Title: Discordant / by Richard Hamilton.
Description: Pittsburgh, PA : Autumn House Press, [2023]
Identifiers: LCCN 2023004986 (print) | LCCN 2023004987 (ebook) | ISBN
  9781637680735 (paperback) | ISBN 9781637680742 (epub)
Subjects: LCGFT: Poetry.
Classification: LCC PS3608.A6945 D57 2023 (print) | LCC PS3608.A6945
  (ebook) | DDC 811/.6--dc23/eng/20230215
LC record available at https://lccn.loc.gov/2023004986
LC ebook record available at https://lccn.loc.gov/2023004987

Cover art: *The Double Soul of Afropunk*, Thomas Sayers Ellis, 2017.
Cover design: Melissa Dias-Mandoly

Table of Contents

"Defense is sight; widen the lens and see
standing over the land myths of identity,
new signals, processes"

—Muriel Rukeyser

"Fascism is the autobiography of a people that renounces political
struggle, makes a fetish of unanimism, flees heresy, and dreams of the
triumph of the easy option, the triumph of enthusiasm."

—Piero Gobetti

In loving memory
of Charlene Mitchell and James and Esther Cooper Jackson,
tireless freedom fighters in the struggle
for human decency and a better world.

Discordant

Dear Self after I Was Dead

Was I condemned to wander
in relative fog, left to jockey with public
convictions about markets on the mend?
No time for pizza or your favorite jam.
Bent, riding into the future
aboard the train, I dreamt
                              of bee-eaters, Turkish
coffee doled out at organization meetings
a disabused clerk, vagrant. I'd hoped it
wasn't rumored remorse for Marxist "failures."
Denial is no way but this. A tacit flamethrower
a kiss. Short shrift arose from a pale environment
of playlists, no one or nothing intended to mock.
How easy is it to kill a future with
                      better strategies—
personal onus—the emergent world
within? A number of hours spent
in the hole, I kvetched.

Area 51

I turn to the Vietnam War and ask for Paradise Ranch on it. Like respect, the glaring omission is an Aretha Franklin gospel blaring in a food desert. There were no aliens in the CIA reports, just a teeming stack of paperwork noting the pulmonary embolism that straightened my outlook. I want the bodies, aliens, the blood clots that formed in my lower limb and moved to my lungs to serve up more history. My brother,

like me, was placed on blood thinners. Had he spoken with a glib nurse, like I had, he might have asked for more than a broken town to reset his clock. Pogroms, like UFO sightings, are best concealed as lore the townspeople are not privy to. He might have seen the U2s flying overhead at 60,000 feet above coursing blood, the bodies that appeared like ants coagulating in the vein of this artificial town I'll refer to as Chocolate City. Bright lights—

Rumsfeld regards them as enemy combatants; terrorists are flashlights of foreign EKGs: women, children, and the elderly. It must be like what happens when fed a steady diet of Molly and applesauce. Death.

More Paradise Ranch on it, please. Everything tastes better with Paradise Ranch, including Mỹ Lai.

Free Black

Free as the blue cold
       frame I constructed.
Free as the recycled
       pane and crow width.
Free as the ochre
       seeds interlocking.
Free as one's hand in
       soil, pigment.
Free as another choice
       moniker, snow years.
Free as when heat
       entrapped, engenders.
Free to bay at the moon
       green shoot.

Free as history's moral
       panic.
Free as in early
       worms to spring.
Free as immoral, rejects
       raced.
Free as the coming frost
       equivalent.
Free as the flood of Chinese
       immigrants.
Free as sallow hinge
       brute weather.
Free as that blanketing white
       sheet music.

Like reds, rose
       of idle mention.
Like black ants, pills
       in a bladed line.

After Revisiting James Baldwin

The price of being white is that you have no history.
Ditties inside civil servitude erupt, bloat into song.
Agitation as mud mouth and silhouette south
        of here. Longer faces

something existential about the national question
        discourse
for war. Revolutionary socialism is not a trigger-
happy communard.

To ease the riotous burden, twist and burn a knob
of ginger. That long, swarthy night of
voter-block coercion couldn't cut us a deal

before the rainmakers, lonesome

gods we sang to. Rent papers flew in epic fashion
through squalid districts.

Elegiac Statement

Inflections turned folky as Elizabeth
Cotten. A sound hole to which history?
To hurl transnational shoes against
a war criminal. Amendments
are but dead letters, a state's right
to tar and feather. Echo the well-worn
entrusted King Cotton. To the British
left-handed comportment. Upside
down strumming heard the transfer
of wealth. To foreign industrialists
war parts, scabs. Futures, sable blue
grass, sacrilege. Pull back the axis
of evil. A winged creature, spread-
eagle on the bloody veranda, strung.

What We Pay For

In that monetized pothole is the subjective life.
A waterlogged rat is buoyant on the jet-black, oily pool.
A petulant swirl with leftover wishes mars the air we
live with. You too can have this if you work hard
enough. Aspiration Boeing. You too can produce
scholars rational as ash, ashes. Crispy subjects.
The pomegranate-wine toast proffered at Martha's
Vineyard was an appeal that fell on bronzed ears. Any
Bill Clinton blushed before knocking back
a few more. To repudiate, the puddle muddles reality
in which we all see something different: land of the free
not blacks and white congeniality, a great many
underwritings, *coochie coochie coo*. Beheaded summer
bluebells mowed down for the Space and Security division.
Irregular slugs interred behind the scenes. $735 million in
weaponry immured us to wages.

Dear Self after I Was Dead, II.

Should the form mean you take me
seriously, Death isn't cruel. It is lakes I see
myself in. Not unlike terrible actors, hoary
before they attempt slapstick. It had a shape
in worlds we rarely source without
economic means. If I was learning
something fundamental about myself
I would take what turned up
on the surface: mottled reflection strewn
with leaves, difficulty. Adolescence,
the long shadow history cast over the dark and
temperamental evoked. Stymied fish passed through.

Digitalia: Sleep Deprivation

Placate Maryland's Eastern Shore.
Twitter hairpin phantoms that
steal sleep, walk around in
wet diapers of manufacture, manufacture

anxiety. Neck bites. Yips. All sensory
detail is radioactive like Nagasaki, Iraq.
A touch fiber-optic
          to stress, nerve endings
a vulnerable girl
traipsed around in. On the ocean floor

dragging netbooks, boy toys
power, she hoped to lose her IP address
the barbarous,
threw rice harvested from her hair
plantation at the enslaved
ship-world.

Hasn't it been proof-positive, easy
to simulate enthusiasm
          for biological attacks?
The state is so civilian. Modern, blue-
black, bulbous limbs, that everyday velvet
tick in the vein, pitter-pattered

to avoid contending with decline
another hand sacrificed on the farm
altar of expediency.

I crawl out of insomnia, plucking
digital quills from the skin.
A bright orange
flower stilled
sticks its
lone delicate neck out
on the windowsill.

Monument

A white burn under hospital lanterns, labor of
bees. Twilight of the infirm, possibly. Death undoes.
Curt stands between the sulking is a wee bit closer to
Diogenes and the sun, darkness recounts. Descends.
At the ER, I believed bread victual, antiphony of
firmament, cowed night. Bonaparte's making France
great again is the prelude to Donald Trump. What
happened? The critic dons a white coat, dubbed.
Is it because we both openly copulated like dogs?
June in its motor mouth. Lately on the gurney I
kept, in the waiting room, what ought to remain
licorice, a private vice. Grip of enumeration
mirror is what, if not, intolerant nature redux, disc?
Naturally, unmentioned in polite company, twinned.
Ontology to patient muzzles in the hours, two dogs.
Poorly, I without bowl or terse statisticians, weather
a querulous god with epidermal needles. The political
ring of white orbs, eschewed. Bees labor, burn in the
sound institution. Twilight in a jackal's ethical claim.
Terrestrial is the unruly body poised for illegal restraint.
Under cloak of likeness is not so much Diogenes but
verily his terra-cotta tub, domicile. His immaterial hub
waters the erudite primed for corrosion. Blind man jesting
such xylophone is grave, simulacrum. Willy's spit benders
yowl in a nurse's voice drunk as a tattered hospital gown.
Zing of the hourly wage, the hum of underlings against.
      Lightning guts the skull
        whose stethoscope does not extend.

Wake

I.

The blanched recruitment table, balancing on its
hind legs at the job fair, excused itself.
Vetting questions squarely, *you're too much*
doesn't mine the stairwell I had to descend
after all, what I perceived was humiliation.
Cribbed and unexpected incidents like paternalism
are routine deaths, billboards pliant as opinions.
A ruddy excuse for the rising cost of a pack
of smokes. Still, further possibilities suggest beyond
the horizon, smog, late sunset over this body of water—
lichen pools, parrot green crawling over a bed
of rusty nails, I dreamt. Against those abandoned
variations, a flock of pigeons cooing on life
support in a fleshy fold of this still larger body
symbiosis.

II.

Workers shorn among anthills and leafy
intersections, the deserted metropolis, sentenced.
Perished in the bottleneck. Some proverbial
grown-ups, tired of fighting, proffered joy
as a solution to market instability, a Western
dread. I dreamt of braided ants, preoccupied
idle, conundrum of chance world-making
carrying empire's prodigy to account
in the pageantry, for worked silk, the last
itinerant blueprint. Such pomp and festive
cast-offs exalted the dead limp of her empress's
garment at once, shading them from the sun.
How else would they inherit the benign
concession, raising this tone-deaf body above
the terra-cotta, dutifully returning it to earth.

Was

I as

un-

Am

eric

an

as
the

bull-
eted

skin

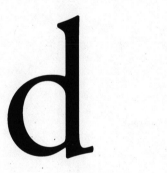

Fred

Ha

mpt

on

live

d

in?

Dream of Chocolate City

a ravine
the unhoused bathe in
primary school   a shitter adjacent

park   0.4 miles
away

what some might
say is   *is* hankering
for clean witness

red phosphorous burns
an upper room   adjacent
          lips   desirous bough's

shot glass   freebase
hard-hard   hard rocks
          hard trips

recompense   got hard
instead   government checks

stayed painting shitty
          views

I stress

stressed workers   couriers in the gig
          economy   night crawlers

                  whose arms rapt
                      of verdant green

          are burning bushes

Audacity

Did I invite this damp
into my life?

Doctor, what camp does the landlord
belong to—the aesthete, the wife?

I went to school, didn't I? Who built
what rival sandcastles, moat

of deviance, from recycled parts?
Would building with one's own

two hands, as if to unhinge
historical context

erase social relations?
Individually I left as much

likely hampered the schoolgirl.
These certain birds keep nesting.

About my head cold, patron.
Virtual energy is Power's poor racket.

The kettle leaves interstitial.
Trace earnings, pocketknife

cut to self-medicate
the wound.

If I am but
a number

divided by two, shouldn't clouds
sunder Christ

       the voyeur needless
baptismal hand?

       We know what makes us ill.
Network-centric individual

       will, irradiation, and class
position to Power. Is it well above

       with you—notwithstanding
below?

Dear Self after I Was Dead, III.

Did society deify individualism?
It was not an accomplishment.
Friendship did not seem dead.
Maybe. It was not bewitched.
Arthur Miller would write about it.
Willy Loman courted death.
Modern barriers are material.
Alienation is a blue spin device.
I did not want to get used to it.
Everyday closeness felt clammy.
Radiation killed pathways to plants.
Feeling was not a recipe for success.
Faregates were constant reminders.
I could hop at my own risk.
We were blued by surveillance.
We bought into living out loud.
Wilding to disarm we jettisoned.
Frequencies killed the nerve.
It undermined the budding of the event.
It undermined true friendship.
A cold apparatus next door greened.
I did not think it seemed unknowable.
Structures were killing machines.
The mind went AWOL just to budge.
It broke at the crack of a pistol fired.
I bled what few resources it stole.
Common winds swept through.

Linear Plane

Lately, I've been reading what stacks up as self-help
detritus, about how we are not in control
about how God is the sole and final judge
of what we need and don't need. Need or don't need is
entirely naive, at best. I mean doesn't it seem
like a deliberately cruel mechanism to quell dissent?
God is a judge. I mean doesn't it seem more likely
a move to disappear social difference, to bask in that
        pixelated glow of free-market love?
Even climate-stricken, natural disasters, one might
        argue, to always be argued,
are the outcome of a human disregard for science,
material concerns, and the environment.

By suggesting one is not an expert or sufficiently
untrained at drawing conclusions about his, her, or
their own life, "professionals" attempt to disabuse us
of the right to name and build a better world.

I should be clear, this is poetry, so far as I can tell.
This is not an anti-vaxxer screed. We are still in the grip
of a pandemic. It is utterly stupid that there are those of us
who'd rather dispense with market options
        for lifesaving drugs.
It reads awfully like the same judge who doesn't care
for bodily autonomy or the material survival
        of certain newborns.

Another Country

Why are people like the worst cyborgs?
Why are we so bent on invasions?
What does privacy mean to you?
Is it a by-product of capitalism?
Are you a punk-ass robot?
Are you an eavesdropping nonevent cop?
Are you that bored and boring?
Do you know where to draw the line?
Are you cowboy forefathers blind?
Are you the child pedophile?
Why wouldn't I say Peeping Tom?
Do you like your vistas raw?
Are you entitled to everything?
Are you white?
Are you a white man who is not white?
Are you into aspiration porn?
Do you see?
Do you see?
Is this just confirmation for you?
Are you stacking your chips?
Are you fondling the crucifix?
Are you some form of reality TV?
Would you like better ratings?
Are you hedging your bets?
Right now, are you hedging your bets?
Are you like Jim Bakker's accomplice?
Are you in it for Jesus?
Are you keeping things safe for poetry?
Would you say an audience of peers is correct?
Would you sell me some spiel about protection?
Why not just say you're a xenophobe?
Why not just say you're a monkey bar?
Where is your sense of personal boundaries?
Only when it pertains to you?
Can we have a borderless country, too?
Can I have my shit back in private?

Or do you like the smell?
Should I call you perverted?
When is it scatologic?
Are perversions reserved for a special few?
Must you trot out all your law enforcement tools?
Can you roll your eyes some more?
Is that your erasure gadget?
Must I call it inspector, too?
Let me guess, you hate white space?
Let me guess, you hate history, too?
What should I do with your microaggressions?
How about some microgreens?
How can I settle your private antics?
How do I cancel your culture queens?
Who should collect your ashes?
What should we do with your incomplete will?
Your incomplete intel?
Why are you so perverted?
Why are you so insecure?
Why hide behind religion?
Why not just say you're a nymphomaniac for Jesus?
Are you a closet variety show?
Why can't you leave well enough alone?
Is it your truth?

What's in a Name?

Like Goldberg, Fritz?   Will it
get you somewhere closer to   industry

execs, will it stamp out consciousness
on Broadway

blackface. What's in Emily Dickinson's
black cake—

will you fit into August Wilson's piano or
Death of a Salesman, into communist

defense of black love, black
initiatives? Is it anything like Reconstruction

Cyrus Briggs? The Paris Commune in Civics
class   all social relations.   Will wars end

behind the glitz   and grammar
the A-list compulsion to unsee? I deprogram

the potential for atomic bombs
the potential for skullduggery
the potential for A. Hamilton

My posse on Broadway that hacked into
the fruit of our labor is worm

to the core. Paul Robeson's celebrity beat on
a horn—

Scottish miners swam, Apollo's warm eyes
sutured dust coal

                    —Ol' Man River
                to the revolutionary church

stateside. Black aster, sleeve of green
apples are canaries

better hushed, not sour or openly crisp
fatal to our distribution maps—

segregation.

Tulsa, 1921

Fireballs rained down from the sky, according
to several eyewitness accounts.

Aerial attacks foreshadowed the 1985 MOVE
bombing in Philadelphia, except the victims.

Media loved the children, so, it could not bear
seeing kids raised like beating hooves

naked limbs galloping in the front yard.
Is that why we bombed the fuck out of them?

Feral, obsessive compulsions with baby
colts, not human impulses wealthy or worthy

of de-
escalation, we murdered.

Eclipsed.

Should not a tally of Tulsan deaths that day
an estimated three hundred, include

what precipitated the massacre, moments
leading up to the event?

Dick Rowland, a nineteen-year-old black shoe
shiner, accused of raping a white woman.

Eclipsed.

Bankers, not porters. Lawyers, not janitors.
Owners, not farmers. Not the indigenous

Muscogee (Creek) Indians we remember
their forced removal.

Amanita Muscaria

Some are addicted to opium, mythologies.
Science, in the same way some are wars.
Santa Claus.

Foraging for surround, mycelium
Rudolph the Red Nose
Reindeer, Bing Crosby's hit—

*It's beginning to look a lot like
Christmas*, Vietnam, napalm, and birches.
Clear the ground hallowed out

by shells, for hallucinogens. Shamans.
Shame, we don't value mulch more.

Dear Self after I Was Dead, IV.

You are not lazy. You are not stubborn. You are not crazy. You are

not ridiculous. You are being hacked. The digital mafia won't let

any of us rest. To you with insomnia, the elderly, the eccentric, the

left. To those who expired young before their arrest. To those with

bodily mutations, atrophied muscles, abnormal limbs, neurological

developments, disorders. You are not a statistic, spurious, naturally

induced. You are not a human palimpsest without root causes.

You are not an individual country, rather caught

in their ugly social experiment. Their regulation, an unwelcome

magnetic hook in your flesh, is a barbarous nation, a stain on the

      public trust.

Dear Professor Nguyen, were there bees about the walls,

the mind? Bees in hollowed grooves, windowsills. I've

grown to hate microwave auditory effect. Does human

perception, the perceived sound haunt? Dead bees I heard like

sudden turns. Like voltas, sudden deaths. Exasperated I, unbother

yourself; it's an imperative I hate, like turning into some bootleg

      version of the elite.

Believe, as it seems, in the Snowden revelations. The post-911,

911. It is after midnight, raining outside, and I've risen

to check the door locks in the apartment now contending

with pelting at the rear of my neck.

The poem never means to instantiate.

It is not a facsimile copy of history.

It is not organized forgetting.

It is not a figment of my imagination. You are dismayed, dis-

sent. Do it for the recluse that was the great Paul Robeson, at the

end of his life, surveilled and awfully discredited. Do it for the

women arrested and tried for sedition, legally harassed, stalked,

jailed, deported, violated. For their children caught in the state's

expansion to quote unquote stamp out terrorist needles in a hay-

stack. Do it against their enterprise, for a growing body of critical

citizens. Balk at the audacity of hope sutured to "inevitable"

measures. It retards. It ticks. It creates problems to solve inadequately.

It drugs. It meddles. It cages. It kills. It hates a thinking subject.

The rev is a posthumous engine era. Wind

at your back. You are not alone. You are not the white noise

you deploy to forget. You are not an emergency exit

nor a happy, uncritical medium.

Were they the routine costs in our supposed freedom?

Object

ob·ject (noun): a thing that forms an element
of or constitutes the subject matter of an in-
vestigation or science as in the *object of study*.
Wartime conflicts bode conflicting shadows.
Some things are cast, foregrounded, while oth-
ers peck through the tumult of darkening back-
grounds. I can be raced and seen. It is through
whose lens darkly. I can be raced and unseen.
Who and what gives it authority?

Just like that. US Air Force C-17 clears the landing during its final
2021 evacuation at the international airport in Kabul, capital city
of Afghanistan, home to the largest percentage of market-opium
in the world. A great deal of human meat discovered in the wheel
well of the transport plane, according to American news syndi-
cates, has me thinking about Saigon, the bloodstained butts of
US military rifles, clobbering the heads of Vietnamese refugees
clamoring for space aboard the aircraft in 1975, the year I was
born. All this talk of flesh remains, gives pause to a feeling subject.
US foreign policy's stomach for war, its exceptional nature, marks
a catacomb of human casualties, a subaltern gallery of the dead,
including women and children.

I would wonder
if an accounting

of the porous body
domestic abandonment

was somehow
to its sister

a transnational context
for war wherein

premature deaths
and disease

pathologized
as individual private

matters waned
as public concerns.

The silences
perfumed.

Innocent and criminal are alien to me. I do, on the other hand,
carry the memory of a young man whose life was colored by a
different form of state terrorism. The Atlanta Public School (APS)

> system, we'd all learn
> was a minefield of Common Core
> Standards where useless adverbs
> *highly* and *effectively* assaulted
> educators and students alike

forced to manufacture intelligence without concern for materi-
al conditions that drive inattention and learning disability in the
classroom. Year after year, attendance numbers fell. Students grew
disenchanted, disappeared. Many more were purged from school
rosters. How many children glint in natural sunlight?

Defiant rays
cut against

the state's
                    apathy, the

                                        charitable
                            bon voyage, the

buttoned-up sense
        that   everything which
         could   have
           been done,

                had. That help, in
    the form of
              military
      aid, support for
          armed
          insurgencies,

     indiscriminate
           killing, that
        polished look

    the infrastructure
     winks

       actors pirouette
          airplanes
   lift-off
 leaving   whole

countries
      devastated
      in the wake.

    ob·ject (noun): something material that may be
    perceived by the senses as in *I see an object in*
    the distance.

Flawed though "state-of-the-art" surveillance equipment, the US
military has long posited that, given the standards set forth in
the laws of armed conflict, there is an acceptable margin of error,

which is to say room for a percentage of unavoidable civilian casualties. Collateral damage. The lives of innocent people, in the quest for freedom and the eradication of terrorist evil, are gambled on, devalued. In June 2016, a strike inside the confines of a crowded area peopled with civilians shopping or milling about in Syria resulted in the death of thirty-four-year-old Abdul Wahab Adnan Qassim. Qsay Saad lost his wife, Zohour; his fourteen-month-old daughter, Aisha; and his youngest son, Abdulrahman, when air raids pummeled a building purported to be harboring ISIS rebels. Missed targets and misidentification are common as noted in a 2018 Joint Chiefs' study as the two leading causes of civilian casualties in American military operations. That said, discrepancies in terms of target intentions and de facto operations in the flow of war are troubling not due to any supposed margin of error (nightmarish enough in its pact with excusable deaths), but that the actors behind the calamity are increasingly worshiped as heroes, purveyors of truth, freedom fighters, and crime busters safeguarded from reckoning.

Always at the root
touching

exposed nerve
                    ganglia of

victims
            maimed

bungled
inside routine

                    operations,

    scuttle of

crossfire attacks, or

mistaken for dead.

In 1998, I would finish a yearlong contract as an intern with Hands on Atlanta (HOA) AmeriCorps where the focus was literacy development for students attending Martin Luther King, Jr. Middle School. The school community was home to a black and working-class neighborhood near downtown Atlanta and the historic Grant Park. Capitol Homes Housing Project, first established in 1941, was not Grant Park's thorny relative, but rather home to an inflow of children and many working adults.

In Grant Park, it was not uncommon to see newlyweds, often white thirty-somethings walking their dogs or spilling out of the newest pub or hipster dive bar. Incidentally, 1998 marked the same year when, under former president Bill Clinton, the United States launched an offensive: a cruise missile attack against camps in Afghanistan that it presumed had holding cells for terrorist campaigns spearheaded by Osama bin Laden, a wealthy Saudi exile. We are told it was a response to the bombing of US embassies in Tanzania and Kenya. It was the preface to a twenty-year war.

> ob·ject (noun): something physical that is perceived by an individual and becomes an agent for psychological identification as in *the mother is the primary object of the child*. Distance from. Closeness to.

The divide felt volcanic to me. Seeing unchecked wealth beside abject poverty was like red-hot magma pushing up. Students of color whose overlapping differences placed them at the margins of multiple identity categories were treated like afterthoughts by most educational institutions. HOA's governing body assigned me to a sixth-grade class, an elective course in beginner's Spanish taught by a Spelman graduate. I was tasked to look after a young man who'd been typecast and drugged for behavioral issues. At the time, Ritalin was the go-to pharmaceutical for children diagnosed with attention deficit hyperactivity disorder (ADHD) or classified by some other neurodivergent mind state. School nurses would administer daily a psychiatrist-approved dose of Ritalin, and, within minutes, he'd be starry-eyed and vacant, flailing his arms, a different kind of challenge. As neurology has it, the brain is complex. I almost never take the position that I know what is best for an individual. Watching that young man, I puzzled over factors that may have shaped his *discordant* will. Many students endured

                    housing insecure
                    arrangements
                    with relatives

                    in emergency shelters.

                    Many more arrived at school
                    having   not

                    eaten
                    ravenous

                    for mediocre   school

                    lunch.
                    It was lunch.

Were students traumatized by viewing wealth inequality on their way to school? How did that impact their ability to sit still, pay attention, hear, and take cues from members of the middle class, albeit schoolteachers living on embarrassing salaries?

Toward the end of my term with AmeriCorps, I would commence looking for jobs at natural food stores. It was the easiest way to pay bills while learning about subjects like sustainable farming, cultural food ways, medicinal herbs, foraging, and more. I would secure a job in the herb and supplement department at a black-owned health food store frequented by the owner's good friend and celebrity, Dick Gregory. Locals looking to stretch their monthly food stamp allotment, opinionated and quizzical, would hover over the exorbitant cost of heirloom tomatoes and locally farmed muscadines. The owner would practically give foodstuffs away.

In 1967, Dick Gregory began a public fast to protest the war in Vietnam, breaking it forty days later, ninety-seven pounds lighter, the story goes, with a glass of fresh-squeezed fruit juice. A tired and work-addled public held stories about how Dick was shot in the knee while protesting at the Watts riots in 1965, how food and food sovereignty, like health and wellness, are tied to the struggle for human freedom. An extraordinary satirist and comedian, Mr. Gregory had an eternal funny bone and benevolent heart.

ob·ject (verb): to put forth in opposition; to say something to express one's disapproval of or disagreement with something.

This must smack in the face of US imperialism, whose signature ammo is a bloated military budget, manufactured crisis, or disaster capital and Cold War flubbing. The Department of Defense could have hired Dick Gregory, the celebrated write-in candidate who garnered 1.5 million votes for US president against political incumbent Richard Nixon in 1968, as committee adviser to lead a budgetary detox against failed wars. The store was located between the affluent Cascade Heights neighborhood and steely southwest Atlanta (home to West End Mall). I would volunteer to organize the stock supply of medicinal herbs, so that I could learn about their usage and memorize common names for plants. I did not last in that position. The store closed not long after I found a new job at a different health food grocer, better organized, making a mere fifty cents more uptown.

Through it all, that young man from the sixth-grade Spanish class
traveled with me. I never forgot the listless look in his eye,

> or the ways he left the
> tarmac of his reality
> on Ritalin.
> Before the fall

> of the Twin
> Towers, the World
> Trade Center,
> I would end up in

> Williams, Oregon,

in spring 2001, an apprenticing farmhand in a program run by
Sara Katz and Ed Smith. The Herb Pharm program, an appren-
ticeship designed to provide hands-on experience in sustainable
farm operations, boasted wide popularity in the natural food in-
dustry. The program housed twelve of us, provided a meager food
stipend for pantry and staple items, and a dream: eight hours a day
on our knees, in the fields amid echinacea and chamomile flowers,
goldenrod and alfalfa cover crop. We would till, weed, seed, build,
turn compost, harvest, cure, dry, and garble medicinal herbs. We
would dig swales with pickaxes and install greywater systems. The
setting was pristine: eighty-three acres overlooking

Applegate Valley.

> I wondered, what if

as Brooks, you

> *sit where the sun*
> *light corrupts*
> *your face*

if

> sandwiched between
> the Siskiyou Mountains

fables fall,   grate

a nationalist
infatuation with the

Zombie Apocalypse,
of late.

One evening, at a nearby farm, I would meet Chi, a local farmer whose apple orchards, strawberry fields, and society garlic made everyone swoon. Interns helped Chi lay out and sort dehydrated apples. Together, apprentices would press the meat for cider. Afterward, each vied for Chi's attention and took to a different part of the farm to pick his brain for details. I had long forgotten the young man's name, who had made a name for himself. An outline of the surrounding downtown Atlanta neighborhood stayed with me: liquor stores, a cemetery, pawnbrokers, abandoned storefronts, and disquieted drunks would emerge like peaks of the Pyrenees Mountains, like they forever belonged, laying claim to the region. What falls back or perhaps lingers in the

shadows
the architects

the school system
If I adjust
the aperture

memory

widening
the lens
a host

of state
agents with
hands in.

ob·ject (noun): a person or thing to which a
specified action or feeling is directed.

The decade that followed saw a standardized testing scandal in
which Atlanta teachers, saddled with felony charges for altering
test outcomes, were placed under investigation. Thirty-four of
thirty-five teachers were black. Some might argue they were bat-
tling their own erasure, feeling the pressure from a school system
that set test score mandates and threatened educators with termi-
nation for poor results.

At the heart of this debacle is an *object of study*
as in ob·jects (noun): things that form an ele-
ment of or constitutes the subject matter of an
investigation or science.

A push for privatized education and the trend in the development
of corporate funded charter schools would emerge as a possible
reason for the near-vigilante takedown of the Atlanta contingent
whose actions mirrored those carried out by educators around the
nation, including the nation's capital of Washington, DC, where
a great many schools were flagged for testing infractions. No pol-
itician will admit that there has been an all-out war, public versus
private, a move to shrink government funding for public educa-
tion and outsource social services to private schools. The adage
you can't see the forest for the trees applies here. Having an explic-
itly racial take on school failures, evidenced by the concentration
on failing schools in districts, predominantly black, where severe
forms of precarity persist, requires a staunch commitment to a
terrible myopia perhaps meant to deflect and bury a more com-
plicated truth.

To ob·ject (verb): to put forth in opposition; to
say something to express one's disapproval of or
disagreement with something.

This young man, his disregard for conformity, like GIs protesting
their forced participation in the Vietnam War, was a paean against
what many military enlistees saw as their invisibility. *Gooks are like
niggers*, one Vietnam veteran posited. *Meat. We don't exist.* Now
account for the tragic number of women and children in their
midst. Repression and coercion, some might argue, are among
those widely held playbook tactics US politicians, lawmakers, and
policy hounds use to advance intervention and justify invasions,
to rationalize institutions of social control.

Chi looked at me and said, with gusto, "viva la revolución!" I read
Spanish and could translate but had little knowledge of the con-
text for his reply. "Have you ever been to Cuba?" he asked "No,"
I said, without hesitation. What followed was reams of informa-
tion on Cuba's movement to address food insecurity on the island.
After the collapse of the Soviet Trade Agreement in 1989, an era
now referred to as the Special Period, along with the tightening
of the US Trade Embargo by a string of US presidents, beginning
with Dwight D. Eisenhower in 1960, Cuba's government turned
to low-input sustainable agriculture to offset food deficits and
augment their tables. The greening of Cuba became synonymous
with my grandmother, a red-dirt Alabamian in the Black Belt,
and the groundswell of largely black southern farmers whose goals
entailed making ends meet by growing their own food.

like ob·jects (noun): things that form an ele-
ment of or constitutes the subject matter of an
investigation or science as in the *object of study*,
our predicaments varied.

Still, no one understood food sovereignty better than the direct
descendants of sharecroppers whose land had been confiscated

under racial terms and divisions, which wrested power from those who inherited years of economic depression, including bank loan redlining.

Years later, being patted down by airport security at José Martí International Airport

I wondered why
Chi never mentioned

racial divisions
or the mountains

grandma, festooned
dusk-colored
climbed

the signposts of
Jim and Jane
Crow

stereotypes
which animate

the   lives   of

black
people
throughout the
diaspora.

Cuban guards
laughing
moving their hips

innuendo
while fishing
through
my luggage
seized all but
my clothing

and duffel
bag of condoms

meant for
distribution

which they'd insist
I'll need apace

card-carrying member
of the *negro* race.

In a country like Cuba, where homelessness is a foreign concept, illiteracy nonexistent, and the concomitant debtors' prison kicked off the island with the likes of US-backed Cuban military dictator Fulgencio Batista during the famed overthrow of US capital and puppet governments in 1959, race codes and colonial influences are troubling relics of the institution of slavery, colonialism, and neocolonialism. It isn't perfect. I often wonder if ideological residues, like racism, live because men, in large part, benefit from them until they don't.

The donning of racial distinctions can and often do lead to penalization. My grandmother deserved forty acres and a mule, to say the least. In Havana, the peasantry, like the descendants of slaves in America, yearned for land. Unlike my ancestors, Cubans, under the leadership of Fidel Castro, met American greed head-on, and, waging an armed struggle for land ownership and property rights, won. Policing in this country started out to prevent slave revolts and uprisings. It quickly evolved into a coercive measure that criminalized vagrancy, that mandated the control of an indigent and inferior group, forcing black people into convict leasing as sharecroppers—a system which reinscribed labor exploitation consistent with restrictive practices perpetuated under slavery.

Historian Dr. Gerald Horne in his book *The Counter-Revolution of 1776: Slave Resistance and the Origins of the United States of America*, describes how enslaved Africans defected, planned, and staged insurrections with the aid of transnational powers like Britain and Spain. Both feudal (Irish, Jews, Gypsies, Slavs) and slave uprisings as well as work-production slowdowns staged by the enslaved, the crowning Saint Domingo Revolution, the abolition of the slave trade in 1807, the emancipation of the enslaved in 1863, and the emancipation during the Civil War comprise the strategies and events that led up to and shaped the transition to a more economical system of capital accumulation. It would be green of me to suggest that we don't make use of and wield our own daily violences. Here I think Frederick Douglass's theory, no war but an abolition war, is an apt way to talk about wartime conflicts, a history from below, and the collective aims of everyday working people living under fascist, capitalist rule.

The great poet-legislator Muriel Rukeyser once said:

> "We are a people tending toward democracy at the level of hope; on another level, the economy of the nation, the empire of business within the republic, both include in their basic premise the concept of perpetual warfare. It is the history of the idea of war that is beneath our other histories."

Racialization and racism have always been critical to empire building. If I were learning something fundamental about myself, I would take, as a starting point, an understanding of the ways in which materialist history, racism, war profiteering, ableism, gender oppression, and economic exploitation shape our reality, granting me the freedom to write on what it means to be human, humanized at the point of political intersections, in life's mix with others.

Having worked over twenty years in education, I find the argument plausible that ADHD is overdiagnosed in black communities, swelling the concentration of black and brown children in Special Education classes. I wonder, however, if the medical establishment blithely ignores how socioeconomic status is central to student success in school. Overcrowding, teacher shortages, and school budgetary cuts mean teachers have little more recourse than to recommend intervention programs. Notwithstanding evidentiary claims about the overharvesting of black and brown bodies for inclusion in Special Education programs, how does one situate what we know about our biological differences, our humanness against the historically racist, Enlightenment-era theorizing of the abhorred place, the "naturally" abnormal or deviant body? That historically situated, "objective" gaze (master/slave) informs our political present wherein many distance themselves from disabled communities. Disability as a social category, not an individual death sentence, opens us to its inherent possibility and desire, the material revaluation of all children.

What does it mean to be human? Educator and disability advocate Wanda Pillow's embodied policy analysis foregrounds the erasure of material bodies in educational contexts, favoring a recognition of bodies whose differentials mark them as unpredictable, leaky, impulsive, intense, messy, and passionate subjects. Furthermore, it critiques widely held views on traditional educational policies which focus on outcomes and standards, providing little-to-no legal protection for students whose diverse differences place them outside the purview of modern-day normative constructs. In her research, Nirmala Erevelles poses the following questions:

> "To whom is public education accountable? Through whose authority are these standards/goals/outcomes de-

ployed? How do these practices of power constitute forma-
tive and deviant subjectivities? What processes are in place
to neutralize and or erase oppositional subjectivities?"

Heteronormative ideology has a particularly salient role in de-
fining the normal child. While there are present day examples of
celebrated identity outliers "living their best life" (queer, bisexual,
and trans, to name a few) by and large, students with sexually
divergent tendencies are almost always still cast out as abnormal,
especially if they inhabit a liminal space—eschew coming out,
are non-visibly queer, are constrained by economic limitations,
are gender nonconforming, or lack normative identity markers.
People are misgendered and misunderstood all the time. At best,
we entertain the notion that they are experiencing what likely
counts as a passing phase in their development, not a true feature.
And more scarily, we insist that discipline (see, punishment) is all
they need to fix their "deviant" behavior. We deride poetry in the
same way we might someone's refusal to go up, come out, adhere
to societal norms, to assimilate, achieve. Fear should be outed.
This is no bland admonishment against personal achievement.
If history is a weapon against abuse and power, then everyone
deserves to be housed, fed, and extended care in a political econ-
omy based on chance, social and economic deprivation, human
exploitation, and erasure. To enlist Muriel Rukeyser, poetry can
be used.

If disability represents a kind of political fault line, then citizen-
ship gets defined by how "normal" one is, how little one deviates
from the ideological norms of the nation-state. If I am drawing
connections, then at the height of Europe's colonialism, charac-
terizing black women and girls as lascivious was a way to reify
the myth of their "uncontrollable" natures, their tendency to-
ward promiscuity and "inherent" proclivity for infidelity, which
ultimately marked black women and girls as property in need of
management or brute training by way of the lash. It is an insid-
ious narrative that lives like a low-grade virus inside the capital-

ist machine and colors how we determine who is most and least deserving of federal support. In a modern context, black women with HIV have been poorly treated (when seen at all) for reasons not too different from their bygone era sisters. To have contracted the virus has meant, among other things, that one is uncultured, complacent, feral, and given their "impulsive" desires, incapable of making sound decisions on their own. In other words, disease is filtered through the notion of individual will versus an accounting of the ways austerity, economic deprivation, housing insecurity, coping strategies that include risk-inclined behavior, labor exploitation, and/or poor education becomes the hotbed or host environment for the development of disease and disability. Disability must be defined broadly!

The notion that Afghan people are backward and incapable of achieving self-determination, in need of exterior aid, would fuel the push for more spending on mechanisms to help deliver civilization to a barbarous nation. It necessitated control by a greater, more dominant, parent-like figure to exterminate the infestation, that is the interior reaches of a country whose signature evil is the Taliban (ISIS, ISIL, ISIS-K, al Qaeda, and others), or "heart of darkness" (to use Joseph Conrad's metaphor). America's invasion would come to be seen as an inevitable intervention, an argument against Islamic extremism or the axis of evil, an invasion beginning with, I should add, former US President Jimmy Carter's 1979 approval of the Mujahideen, the proxy war against the socialist government in Afghanistan and anti-Soviet clandestine mission to stamp out communism. As with most children, like the young man in Atlanta, alternative treatments, intra-communal mediation, expanded forms of basic welfare, harm reduction, natural or holistic medicine, and even a hands-off approach is too much to ask of a nation hellbent on meddling in, imposing, and shaping the affairs of others, especially poor others whose lives one feels are best suited for intervention, enforced compliance, and criminalization.

One might be wondering how all these various thematic threads fit together, having little patience for literary patchworks so perversely stingy or unpredictable in their turns. What else could there be but a toothy tapestry that snakes about to address the exceptional and bombastic breath of US imperialist hegemony, so callous, so bent on institutional control, so committed to oligarchies and to fattening the coffers of the rich at the expense of working and poor people, and the earth. At a time when the US is witnessing a spike in low wage work and a rise in homelessness, legal initiatives that criminalize young people (the great majority of which are black and brown youth), the development of unaffordable housing, the disappearance of federally funded emergency resources, including Medicaid for millions of people, the US is busy rallying support for the current proxy-war against Vladimir Putin's Russia. $886 billion in a proposed budget to the Pentagon and nuclear weapons work at The Department of Energy this year. $877 billion accounted for in a 2022 US military budget. That does not include taxpayer resources siphoned from American working people and into the pockets of gun and weapon lobbyists. According to a report from the National Priorities Project at the Institute for Policy Studies, the average unwitting taxpayer spends $1,087 per year on weapons contractors. For perspective, a mere $270 on average is spent for K-12 education and $6 annually for renewable energy. Where are the priorities? It should come as no surprise that the focus is on geopolitical US domination, which requires a commitment to a culture of forgetting. We must forget how and why these issues matter. And history, especially critical race theory, disability justice, economic class warfare, gender difference, climate science, artmaking, and labor resistance are all under attack because of the kinds of anti-imperialist, pro-working-class, brightly artistic cartographies they serve up. There is nothing more threatening than an informed citizen.

> ob·ject (noun): the goal or end of an effort or
> activity as in *the object of the game.*

Inside the post-9/11 imagined community created by the US nation-state is a fictive vision in its singularity. Dissent is discouraged. Patriots are celebrated as virtual police against world terrorism. To the extent that women enlist in the military to fight these wars, they do so inside a hypermasculine framework. If there is a bone to pick, it is not with men and women who enlist to provide for their families, but rather with the apparatus that is the military industrial complex (MIC), empire. China is not "our" bogeyman. "Our" interests could not possibly have much to do with strengthening the US-NATO-EU alliance, to encircle big bad Russia, as some politicians would have us believe. Imagine how empty and kooky that must sound to single mothers grappling with the rising cost of fuel, diapers, or a gallon of milk?

Time interred under
apartheid-like
punitive measures
in school, I imagined
that young man
built himself a boat
out of
social isolation and
bureaucratic disregard
paddled out
to the water's farthest
reaches
under cover of night
the stars
to commune
with his people—
night garlanded
song.

Where the domestic outflanked all things foreign, I predicted we would begin a war. Before banked fears of fellow citizens are this season's violet denizens—the earth alone. Like spirit murder, the bar so low set mitigates "disruption." A riot is heard. Limb of fire to laminate heaven, we breathe, at the social intersections.

Leave for Cider

That waste of skin is cosmetic defects.
That bed of bad apples whose outer

layer is rich in magnesium soothes
our tired muscles, Chi says.

Transfer those at the edges.
Grab the blue tarp, receding.

See, both rotten and sweet. The sort
even humans talk to, the earth as we are

dying, Chi says. Look for the last
evening light. It is not rose-quartz

sky, the way farmers grapple
with young bad apples.

Race for Funding

Do we measure the wrong things?
What theories do we hold about addiction?
Usage is about pain reduction.
Emotional pain is real.
Historical trauma is valid.
We are not post-racism.
We are not talking heads.
Pain comes in many forms.
Pain can be addressed.
Pain management can be redressed.

White supremacy is a form of sociopathy.
We must lie about these world views.
Marianne Faithfull. Lady Day.
Opioids are chemicals of love.
For some.
The chemical reaction is inherently relational.
Harm reduction is one approach.
Abstinence is another.
Please, do not revive D.A.R.E.
Do we want users to live?

Human Lights

for Hasani Jennings

I wrest angel-

dust from my breast

      pocket

miss the burning

cast-iron Boy-White

leaves on the stove.

I wrest

these lines:

"repeat nonviolent

drug offenders" from

my red tattered mini-

tablet all marked

up with notes

to myself about

recidivism. I'm back

here for "expecting

mothers shackled"

and "transferred

across Alabama

state lines."

For their babies

and something more

I scribbled outside

the margins.

I wrest

another letter

from our kitchen

table, the night our

lights blacked out.

Demolition

Whose business is it
to amplify

human
error ahead

of schedule, wander
into snowy woods, self-

assured as cardinals?
Songbirds could

exhibit A
or B, or nothing

in between natural
progression

city developments
or fledgling.

Morning mitigated
I meet the animal

of her soft body
poor lighting

with burrs.
Makeup fades

on the urgent
face. Buzz

cut against trees
denuded

of their leaves
hungry youth

shuttered, braced:
Elevator pitch

dead branches
dumb laymen are akin

to asking
whose business

is it to disinter
ordinary springs;

opium-addled
black women

from an ice-cold
Anthropocene?

Fruit.

Sleep Talking

I ran into Thomas the other day and felt bad because there are no state or federal responses to the ending of emergency unemployment assistance benefits for millions of Americans. Benefits expired in the District. Thomas hit the streets to fuel his drug habit and feel human. I am unsettled about so many things, including a job I don't have to sacrifice my dignity for. The sub teacher thing, while great in terms of offering employees that proverbial flexibility, is really a shit job because what it means is that you are almost never prepared to succeed at it and kids and everyone else are already oriented to your failure and their respite from failing public school education because such days are considered outs for them, ripples or fissures in an already broken system. Staff rarely listen but will do so if you adopt the right finesse or cinematic Joe Clark, which these days I am loath to muster because my disability is always at the periphery, commanding attention and presence and calm.

De Facto

War pigs hackney a response.
In other words, the stanza stultifies
at times. I need a break from all high-step injunctions, trotting
out routine operations. Killing sprees. Killing
fields.

Cambodia. 1969.

Mason-Nixon lies.
Henry, right in the kisser. *Anything that flies*
on anything that moves. Orders.

Who will suffer the dead—a mouthful
of blood and vomit, lobelia
flowers to dilate the lungs?

Our challenges lie

in *the price and the promise of*
citizenship, conferred, at first, on us,
Mr. President, in 1776, your grateful lot
of heathens—three-fifths human being, we so humbly
contest. This still wet Constitution and ankle
bracelet, monitoring

perverse as Andrew Jackson's Removal Act
of 1830, the indigenous would situate.
As in fig leaves, hagiographies

Lincoln's repatriation
of the formerly enslaved
in 1863, amid southern mercenary indifference,
is what if not placation?

Let the dead spit up Cow Island
the experiment jiggers down Jefferson
until nightmares like we come true.

Come through, Mr. President.
Come true. Come clean.

Invectives

You, *you* with the powder blue sky, the Lenny
Kravitz farts, the Lisa Bonet complexity on set
after set. You mustn't be anything like Tempestt
Bledsoe, Afro-modernist haircut reality whose air
space is off-limits, You Americans mustn't be
flown in. You have been forewarned. Don't you Louis
Armstrong me. Not your Nkrumah, Lumumba casualty
RBG, Senator McCarthy Cult of Personality
skidding on your Texas toast. You, *you*
Madeleine Albright, you Osama bin of useless
Arab children, half-million black right before
the offensive attack (worth it?). Aberrant
90s solipsism, the fuck. I object. You wet
dream of Clinton's "don't ask, don't tell"—Fuck you.

*

Sweet a mojito from their eyelids
stiff with ghoulish memory

armed and at the ready, you
thought, until civilian clothing
next to his locker mate, combing
her hair, lukewarm rendering a
glare in his direction, dependent
motions, half-mast, open to the

reflection in their mirrors
blaring Depeche Mode
insecurity—nuance until
as he turned, the gun you
didn't see, in the dream
        on himself.

*

You who should be given poor to little
photosynthesis. Light deficits, fin for
feeling. Anagram of possibility in the undertow
of your exceptional nature, perforate predation
upon predation. Satan for Santa and Mumbai
rubbish littering the surface to oxygenate dark
asthmatic lungs. Plankton scales and glass
teeth of gritty children who did not
make it out. Sexual
parasites and manageable bites of freedom
to choose how we drown

combing ocean floors, bioluminescent
stalk, illicit grief.

*

You give us frayed edge, distressed institution
of marriage, denim wear, and overturned
sodomy laws as the extent to which we
acquiesced to our own bodies or clean hems
singular unsung articles of clothing that
we'd all kill for. Piled rights to our own plank
and blindfold,

chattel. That said, is there no better form of self
expression, sailor liveries, liberation that
doesn't end with extraction? Pending uplift
what purchase does *Appeal* sew into the lining?
Mutiny flashlights the artery.

Rote Inclination

for Kent Johnson

Innocents twenty-four hours a day, the NSA
are gizmos, examiner. Like surgeons
studying the fix, they dream

of highways, the opposite, again.
To stem left divergence, they scrape
at brain waves. INNOCENTS, the moribund

world, FOR SYNCHRONICITY (ta-da!).
April snows in a glue gun, thought control.
Or, a red wheelbarrow. Study the fix.

Left obsessions, junk drawers.
Elevators emptied at Kalamazoo.
Innocents twenty-four hours a day, the NSA

that twitchy data rope is morass to
the first amendment. Am I black noise?
Studying the fix, they dream

of Clotilda, slave ship radio
waves. They bend black objects, surveil.
In the road of history, the fix
harvesting subaltern dreams.

In a Fix

What makes the allure of whiteness so powerful?
Smoke-black plumage, crows—is it the supposed
promise of material comfort, extralegal
protection from the worst forms of economic
precarity? Blank dreams, all this moxi-
bustion, paraphernalia, buskers in the loo. Barry,

how could you? The Lehman brothers
bargained bonded labor
in antebellum America's South.
What of those vaulted ceilings, Alabama
holdings, protection for the Lehman family
zoo?

Lines

My brother with boils on his scalp
bright spots, intermittent anger, the disease
which drinks itself to death. Jaundice, no one knew

propagates out of sight in prison
colonies behind liquor stores, boarding
rooms full of dark men. Here, things

like Jaundice, are left to fester.
Bright yellow pus seeps out
      of its trap. Out of sight, antecedents
are more like fugitives.

Scars my brother takes with him
to caseworker and trap house
consumed by rose bushes, neighborhood
watch signs. To death,

Jaundice is a boy grown
out of sight in prison
      colonies, the changing
same, scars my brother takes
with him, to caseworker

after caseworker, the trap
      house consumed
by rose bushes, escapes.

Adjectival

Descriptors are worn like army men.
As a boy, I wore, to my chagrin,
a monkey suit from a locally run outlet.
Not that it was purchased on layaway
but that it never fit. I hated it. God bless
my father. America is one savage
constitution in a bowl. Not for the obvious
reasons. Sitting presidents extol virtues
like *finance* capitalism. The longer we live
the more Keynesian our trip. I am against
sanctions. To be clear, wealth drips
down Queen Anne's Lace Street.
Wild carrots in the economy.
Wild carrots on a stick dangle
like slow reformations.

Innards

They—prisoners of war,
song of oblation
along the intestinal wall
as armature, as Ho Chi
Minh. Huey P. Newton's wicker
chair as misnomer, Võ Thị Sáu's blood
against Voltaire's
enlightenment. Polyps. Kings, those
agents of progress. The optical
contusion, exhumed song
of incandescent bloat.
Greening anti-colonial, anti-
in the suicidal ideation. Their
revolutionary mouth, rectum
is beginning continuation.

Claims to the Motion of Life in a Post-War Period

for Bigger Thomas

Impossibility acts terribly like
a ghost declarative, riot act, division.

Chambermaids, kitchens: all things actors
tricked. Black and white distinctions cleave

to branches, jezebels, hicks. Displeasure
acts terribly like an invisible, twinned

entitlement to legal protection. If
real, Bigger is something like Black

Mouth. Lip-cut sedition, black
defilement. If framing it, possibly

innocent (even if he done
wrong), others seen manifold

lock of hair, prepaid minutes, more time
for liberal concessions, adrenaline

a chance to become nigger-
rich, should we survive it—

artillery notwithstanding, white sheet
music as federal troops retreat.

White camelias. Holes. Pistol licks.
Weeping children, the fields.

Southern black families crowded into
their black belts. Belief in the word

for scarce, scarcity, scary, pending
scarification, or the biblical switch.

Rail Against

Bigger is the third rail, boiling coffee—
Natchez to Chicago
magnolias, strike. Toward his family, an attitude
of iron reserve, for which railroad workers strike
a nerve. We the people, many
million in nonconformist labor today
refuse to return to unethical work. Strike!
Invisible as a tree with no standing.
Invisible as war crimes—

overharvested negroes on the front lines
killing other negroes.
Black workers whose fealty you
exploit, object. St. Louis as beeswax, resin
the pigment—encaustic, kept molten on heated
palettes.

Democratic Vistas

after Walt Whitman

To those wealthy who think, "I'm going to
offload the risk of contracting this virus to
those who can't afford to stop working"—
well, for a moment a smidgen of NeNe
Leakes, her vicious civic activism is an
ancillary celebrity tweet, the all too
customary tool. I'll admit, I'm convinced.
There couldn't be, a more democratizing
wing than a violent bleach, a breach
artificial sally   across the
Continental Divide, deracinate.
The settler mind is full of civilizing
          flowers,

fleets. Reality. Cherry blossoms right here in
DC. I admit to tracking today, flowers off-
track, unemployed, and poorly revised.
Form is so Three-fifths Compromise, brute
contract
and gig economy. I couldn't resist the
tryst, handcuffed to an Uber daddy
moment, westward-ho, contingent. Ticket
amnesty, mayoral birding while penning
celebrity
laws·that ding for traffic citations
drivers traced and relegated.
Democracy, could you grant me
a stay from occupation of my nerve
endings? Sally

Hemings, on the one hand, if you please.
In the abstract
          tease. Sally
the subject that was no subject is the way we

misread routine. Penalty in favor of
orangutan flowering—

no person in the social or legal sense.
Property. Be as it may, the self-contract
the domestic ignites. I know I'm
crossing histories. Divides. Just for a
moment
the gilded toilet's empire, so Aristotle
orange man in cleats.
Do celebrate the state's humanity
their lexicon for great big favors
monosyllabic democratizing

ring, ring, ring. Freedom is such a coffle
indiscrete as democracy's minions
sweeping Stadium Drive. Critics are
generally, of one mind regarding what
happens. Sally
forth the multitude of plebs
sniggers,   incredulous, flowering
like offal, worse than senseless things.
Innards contract at the mockery,
patricians as commoners crowd the
streets, momentary derision for mass
gatherings. I might add Caesar's celebrity

status is the reorganization of power
relations, slack. If we bury the
celebrated alive, our surplus
democracy's horizontal lines, a many-
headed Sally multiplies, springs forth, so
dressing Karl
Marx,

Claudia Jones, and Beah Richards
flowers
in a multifarious sea. We contract
momentarily, which

given the perfidy a moment
ocean as insurgent space, celebrate
the profligate, essentials. In abeyance
democracy afloat with
commoners and thieves pirating
wins, the
worker bees we relegate, sally
across a dark
service sector, florid rulings
contractual suffering.

To those wealthy who think, "I'm going
to offload the risk of contracting
this virus to those who can't afford to stop
working": a cagey wager's smock and bent.

Portal

for T. Cherry

Doors—because they had no home—
you stepped right

through them, leaving a toy sex
earring to snag their ruddy navel.

Did you forget
something in the water snake heel

to upward mobility? Reality is whiter
now. Wearing off, they are here

as always, entrance.
Is that not worth noting

how they frame your success
and climb?

They heard vitriol in minimum
wage job solutions as proof

that winter people
were sleeping. On subway

platforms, doors
because they had no home.

It got so you didn't
like the easiness of animal.

Flailing, you
tore at their dopey flesh.

Are not we all more
like servants, underdeveloped

countries clawing
for interior resources?

Don't we all pay
an exorbitant tax

rent?

Speculation

On the blue
line to Largo, it is a ton of scrip and tokens.

The train conductor makes decisions that will
cost us our lives. The incentive to toy with

a tuft of hair as the train car rollicks like green
horses full of soft hardware is probably black.

It is entirely up to you. I am not helpless.
I want to. The lady next to me is screaming

behind the lip of a pink hoodie: "I hate
black niggas." Then, she spits. Someone

drops their crystalline amulet when I board
the next railcar, speculative as we pass U

Street/African American Civil War Memorial/
Cardozo station—

Incoming Light

smokes half-wasted, transit cops
phases of Reconstruction Poetry
celibate as black fidelity turning
the page into itself splays nothing
like individual violence
on the digital dashboard
to gas stove compression
garment I squeeze over routine
swelling like a coffee house
of insider intimacies, teal-colored
virtual tangerines. I wish I'd had
like money to grant Phyllis Hyman
grace, emerald cuts
I could never turn into myself.
Afghanistan, I learned, is bodied
with mines. Peopled. No longer for sake
of poetry I wish I had time
to measure blood army's military
withdrawal. Instead, I fidget as war
trains incoming light, casualties
coalesce abroad. I burned myself
bumping into becoming
what others hated. Writhing there
cold, night's mauled
subjects asleep beneath train
cars ablaze with holes.
Like peregrine
falcons, birds of
prey, one after the other
we flew.

I couldn't have heard
you without killing the first-
person. Squawking into
squawking is the relevant noise
campaign I put down, the self
in writing. Linger
for the sake of poetry. Someday
soon there'll be no room for sun-
dried tomatoes, that wild coyote
we heard they found in Lincoln
Park, skies I source for holes.

Cessation

in the year of the water tiger

Piddling about, I am told, is what
the improvident do.

I want to turn over and face you
like a new leaf, forget the
other side, sleep comfortably in
the dark. Remarkable how I can be so
radiant, printed with hinterland grasses
housed indifferently.
On the ground, being told I am stained glass,
I am forever burning
rocks wrong on the foil. But isn't that
exactly beautiful—

be an old broom, bristles,
having caught heck, headed
for refuse over
and over again.
The repetition is part pattern
manufactured handle, fist-polished
aspersion.

That she and god
could boast a hit of crack
call home the complex hallway
isn't for paperwork.
Had they someplace to go?
Would you offer them
your garrison of fern
crowding, bugs, children
asleep in their quiet wood?

Inci
den

tally
I am

her

e.

Notes

The italicized line in "Audacity" is from Bertolt Brecht's poem "A Worker's Speech to a Doctor."

In "Tulsa, 1921," I refer to the bombing of the MOVE organization and residence in Philadelphia spearheaded by then Mayor Frank Rizzo. It had been rumored that the children, under the leadership of John Africa, were being raised like a pack of wolves; law enforcement's justification for the bombing was the children's "savage" mistreatment. Blame, in this instance, can and should be apportioned. "Hooves" then is the trope I am using to play up that concern.

The italicized line from "Amanita Muscaria" is a line taken from Bing Crosby's song of the same name, "It's Beginning to Look a Lot Like Christmas."

The reference to bees in "Dear Self after I Was Dead, IV." is taken from Diana Khoi Nguyen's poetry collection, *Ghost Of,* as paean to her deceased brother.

The following articles and books were invaluable when crafting the hybrid poem "Object" and informed much of the work:

Anania, Billie. "The Photographers Who Captured Russia on the Eve of Its Revolution." *Hyperallergic.* September 2, 2021.

Bernstein, Sharon. "Explainer: Marijuana pardons in U.S. help thousands, leave others in prison." *Reuters.* October 9, 2022.

Brooks, Gwendolyn. *In the Mecca.* Harper and Row Publishers: New York, NY. January 1, 1968.

Brown, Joshua. "Historians and Photography." *American Art.* Vol. 21, no. 3 (2007): 9-13.

Erevelles, Nirmala. *Disability and Difference in Global Contexts: Enabling a Transformative Body Politic.* Palgrave Macmillan. November 16, 2011.

Freeman, Ben and Hartung, William D. "Unwarranted Influence, Twenty-First-Century-Style: Not Your Grandfather's Military-Industrial Complex." *TomDispatch.* May 4, 2023.

Gerber, David A. *Disabled Veterans in History.* University of Michigan Press. June 6, 2012.

Goodman, Amy. "Dick Gregory in His Own Words: Remembering the Pioneering Comedian and Civil Rights Activist." *Democracy Now!* August 21, 2017.

Grundhauser, Eric. "A Short History of Area 51's Shady Expansion." *Atlas Obscura.* September 16, 2015.

Haiphong, Danny. "War is a Racist Enterprise." *Black Agenda Report.* September 1, 2021.

Hayes, Robin J., director. *Black and Cuba.* 2015. 1 hour and 21 minutes.

Horne, Gerald. *The Counter-Revolution of 1776: Slave Resistance and the Origins of the United States of America.* NYU Press: New York, NY. April 18, 2014.

McCoy, Alfred W. "From Free Trade to Prohibition: A Critical History of the Modern Asian Opium Trade." *Fordham Urban Law Journal.* Vol. 28, no. 1 (2000): 307-349.

McHarris, Philip V. "Why We Have Police: Race, Class, and Labor Control." *Literary Hub.* August 4, 2021.

Nguyen, Viet Thanh. *Nothing Ever Dies: Vietnam and the Memory of War.* Harvard University Press. April 11, 2016.

Powell, Sherlyn Ezell, Eileen Welch, Dan Ezell, Colleen E. Klein, and Linda Smith. "Should Children Receive Medication for Symptoms of Attention Deficit Hyperactivity Disorder?" *Peabody Journal of Education*. Vol. 78, no. 3: (2003).

Rubin, Barnett. "Testimony on the Situation in Afghanistan Before the United States Senate Committee on Foreign Relations." *Council on Foreign Relations*. October 8, 1998.

Rukeyser, Muriel. *The Life of Poetry*. Wesleyan University Press: Middletown, CT. September 1, 1996.

Stapp, Katherine. "United States: Black Children Often Mislabeled as Hyperactive." Inter Press Service. April 25, 2000.

Stein, David. "The Untold Story: Joe Biden Pushed Ronald Reagan to Ramp Up Incarceration—Not the Other Way Around." *The Intercept*. September 17, 2019.

Umi, Vaughan. "Shades of Race in Contemporary Cuba." *The Journal of the International Institute*. Vol.12, issue 2 (2005).

Watson, Eleanor. "Human Remains Found in Wheel Well of U.S. Military Aircraft That Departed Afghanistan." *CBS News*. August 18, 2021.

Zeiger, David, director. Griego, Evangeline; Zarrow, Aaron; and Zeiger, David, producers. *Sir! No Sir!* 2005. 85 minutes.

In "De Facto," italicized lines in the third stanza refer to orders from former president Richard Nixon amid the bombing campaign in Cambodia. In the fifth stanza, "the price and promise of citizenship" is taken from former president Barack Obama's 2009 inauguration speech.

The penultimate line of the poem "Invectives" contains a reference to David Walker's four-part pamphlet *Appeal* first published in 1829.

Acknowledgments

I am grateful to poet Evie Shockley for selecting *Discordant* as the Center for African American Poetry and Poetics' 2022 book prize winner. Evie's experiments in poetry and art world-making hold a sable light to what gets elided, sanitized, or left out of conversations about contemporary American poetry. She does so with tremendous feeling, formal inventiveness, and concern for the material conditions that dog so many of us both in the US and abroad. Her faith in the arc and tilt of my writing grants me that warm feeling of being in the presence of good company. Thank you, Evie!

This book is supported in part by a grant from the Arts and Humanities Fellowship Program in Washington, DC. Immense thanks to Anacostia and Mt. Pleasant library staff and building maintenance employees in DC for putting up with me! Public libraries remain one of this nation's greatest equalizers and grounding hubs for all people.

I am grateful to my grandmother Margaret Clark whose tough spirit and sobering love I believe informed parts of this book's construction. Thank you, Tish and Adam Turl of *Locust Review*, for championing my writing, for your sharp criticism, love and material support. Thank you Kwoya Fagin, Jamal Jones, Terra Olivera, Natalie Kram, Stewart Shaw, and Mikahl Linweber for constant words of encouragement. Grateful for the editorship and advice of poet Martha Collins. Huge thanks to Luther Hughes, founder of Shade Literary Arts in Seattle. Thank you to the brilliant poets francine j. harris and John Keene for sitting with the manuscript and writing blurbs given the ever-greater squeeze on all our time. The cover art would not have been possible without the artistic eye and precision of poet and photographer Thomas Sayers Ellis. Steffan Triplett, in no uncertain terms, thank you for believing that this was a collection that needed to see the light of day. A friend once told me to kiss my editors! Thank you, Christine Stroud, editor in chief at Autumn House Press.

Cornelius Eady, cofounder of Cave Canem and legendary poet, has been a virtual life jacket and source of inspiration to me. Thank you for all the silent ways you continue to enrich the lives of black poets and all fledgling writers. Big shout out to poets Cedric Tillman, Gina Dorcely, Honorée Fanonne Jeffers, John Keene, Jericho Brown, and Tyehimba Jess for your support leading up to and during the COVID-19 pandemic. So too, there are countless others who remain anonymous and are no less deserving of my gratitude. Thank you, all.

Author Bio

Richard Hamilton (pronouns: he/they) was born in 1975 and grew up in Elizabeth, New Jersey, and Columbus, Georgia. His first book, *Rest of Us*, was published by Recenter Press in Philadelphia. A Cave Canem fellow, his poetry has appeared in *Consequence*, *Steel Toe Review*, *Rigorous Magazine*, *128 Lit*, and *Obsidian*. Hamilton holds an MFA in poetry from the University of Alabama and an MA in Art Politics from NYU. He is the recipient of the 2023-2025 CAAPP creative writing fellowship and lives in Pittsburgh, PA.